A NURSE'S STRESS RELIEF COLORING BOOK

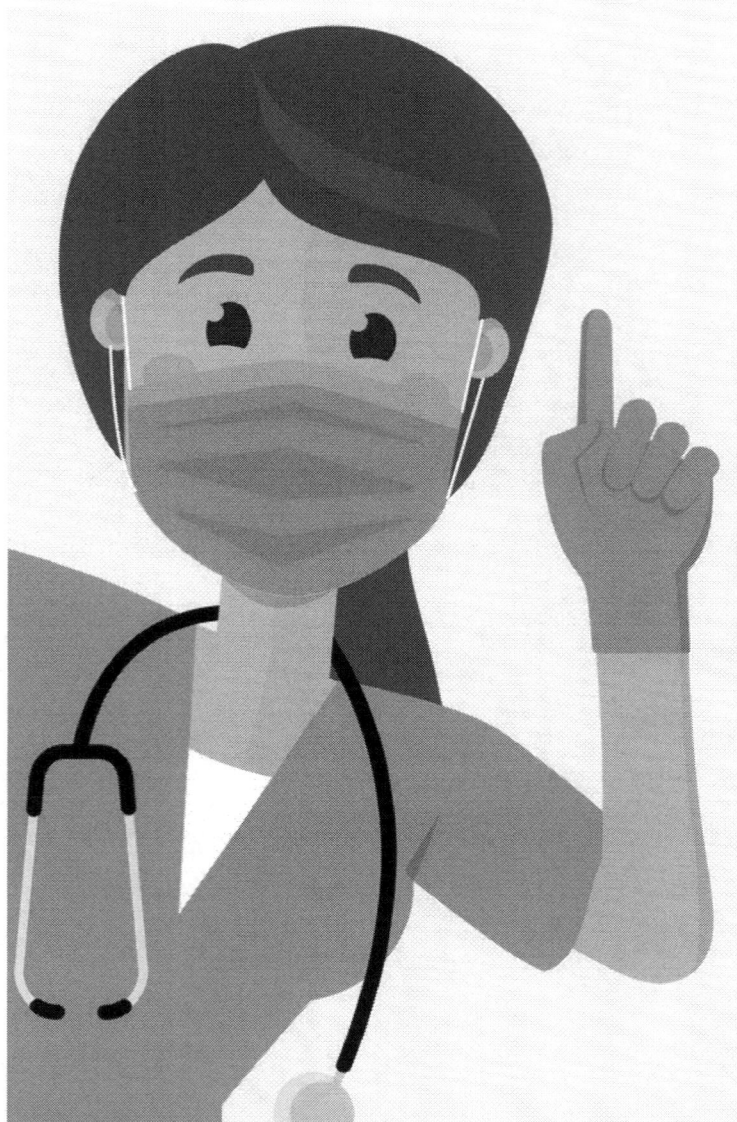

This Book Belongs to :

_____

_____

_____

Introduction

To the Superheroes in Scrubs,

Every day, you selflessly give so much of yourselves, often forgetting to take a moment just for you. This coloring book was designed with the incredible world of nursing in mind, allowing you to reflect on your journey and find moments of peace amidst the chaos. Dive into these pages, let your creativity flow, and remember to always make time for yourself. Here's to the healing power of colors and the relentless spirits of nurses everywhere.

xoxo, Jolie Joy

Copyright © 2023 by Jolie Joy

No part of this book may be used or reproduced in any manner whatsoever without the prior written permission of the author.

For free resource visit

www.thatslovepublishing.com

Nursing is love in Scrubs

Smiles Bring Comfort

Love in Action

Caring makes Miracles

Nursing where miracles happen

Hearts Heal Souls

Through Compassion we Heal

Restoring Hope Daily

Nurses Advocate

Earth's Healing Angles

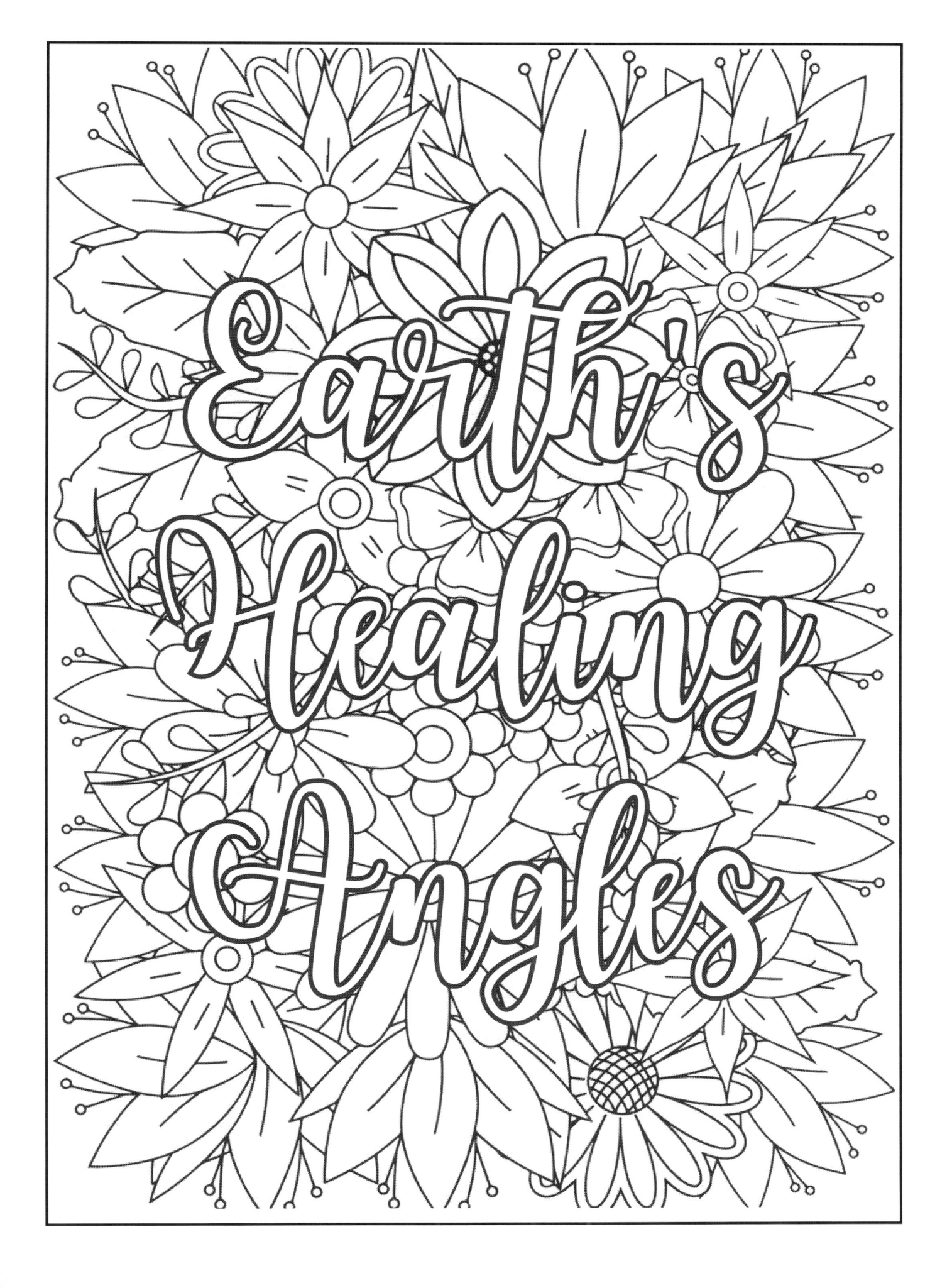

Whispers of Courage

Illuminating Lives With Care

Nurse by Choice Caregiver by Heart

Where Love and Science Meet

A Journey of Heart

Nurse Life

Healers in Motion

Compassion in Action

Nurses bring Comfort

Nurses make a difference

Care with a Smile

A World Of Care

Nursing is my Calling

Nursing where kindness matters most

Caring Hands, Healing Touch